School Interview Practice:

Interview questions and exemplar answers for 11+ and 13+ entrance interviews.

<u>A note from the author.</u>

A growing number of independent schools now include an interview as part of their entrance requirements, whereby they meet and talk to potential students wishing to join their community. The reasoning behind this is simple: they wish to accept not only the brightest students but those who are also articulate, confident and who have an interest in the world they live in.

Interview questions can be broadly categorised into types, from those which are designed to ascertain a prospective pupil's attraction to the school and others which elicit information about the student's own hobbies and interests to those which indicate the scholar's understanding of wider issues and affairs both nationally and internationally.

This text has been designed to give a flavour of the types of questions which may be asked at interview, together with suggestions as to why each question might be asked – you might wonder what information the interviewer hopes to glean from asking the question. Every interview question is followed by three exemplar answers, one which is judged poor, a second which is good and a third which is excellent. Each answer comes with a commentary which indicates how an interviewer might note each response together with hints and tips for making the answer even better.

Over the course of my twenty plus years in the world of education, I have held many senior roles including that of Deputy Head, Academic Director, Examiner and Non-executive Director. I have developed a strong understanding of what interview questions children have been faced with from a huge variety of schools. I have personally prepared many students for their school interviews with the pleasing result that as well as gaining acceptance to their preferred institution, the child has usually enjoyed the experience having become familiar with the questions and gained an understanding of the process as a whole.

The important thing to remember as you prepare your own son or daughter for an interview is that the staff want to get to know them – they are not trying to trip students up or to trap them into giving silly answers. The best schools spend a lot of time creating a friendly and welcoming environment where a child can feel comfortable and thus gives the best impression of themselves during their interview.

This book is designed to give you the tools to prepare your child for success at interview. I hope you enjoy familiarising your child with the interview process and that they gain entry to the school of their choice.

Best wishes,

Anna Wheatley

Why do you want to come to 'X'?

This is a question which candidates are typically faced with early on in their interview. The worst answer I have ever heard is "because my mum wanted me to come here". This is a very poor answer because it shows that the child has no understanding of what that school is offering and that they have no hunger to attend the establishment. This would automatically make the interviewer feel negatively towards the family. A better answer focuses on what is individual to that school, a reason why the child feels they would be a good fit and even better, if they indicate how they can contribute to the school itself.

Let's take a look at some possible responses.

A poor answer.

It's close to where I live and a lot of my friends are hoping to come here.

This student shows no indication that they know anything about the school at all in terms of the facilities they have, the subjects on offer or their extra-curricular offer. The fact that the school is located close to where they live is a good reason for choosing the school but not one the school wants to hear. They want to know that the child is aware of the school's reputation, their sporting triumphs, their academic success and excellent examination results. This student is focused only on the practicalities. In addition to suggesting that they want to attend the school as it is near to their home, they also cite the fact that their friends are also applying. At best, this shows the popularity of the school and that the child is sociable, hoping to join with their friends. However, this could also indicate a reluctance to venture into a new situation without the knowledge that their familiar peer will be accompanying them, suggesting a nervous disposition and a reluctance to take the lead. Some schools are looking specifically for children with leadership qualities, an answer like this hints at a subservient nature and a child who is a follower.

<u>A good answer.</u>

I found the building really impressive with the imposing entrance hall. The sporting facilities and coaches really attracted me because I'm really good at cricket and football – I play cricket at county level and am in the first team for football at school. I'd really like to take advantage of the opportunities offered here, possibly trying out some of the sports that are new to me like table tennis and fencing as I think I'd enjoy them.

This is a better answer as the child has mentioned something specifically about this particular school. Even a simple, pleasant reference to the physical appearance of the school will make the interviewer feel positively towards them. There is then a clear understanding of the provision offered by the school suggesting an element of research and comparison with other schools, together with the comments suggesting why this school is particularly well suited to them. They have slipped in the fact that they play sport to a high level, giving the interviewer a subtle indication that they could be an asset to the sports department. They also create an aura of confidence by referring to the fact that they are keen to try a sport which is completely new to them, showing that they are not afraid to try new things and in fact will embrace the opportunity to discover more about themselves and their abilities. Overall, this answer would create a favourable impression of the student, who has shown a clear, specific interest in the school and what it can offer in addition to hinting at what qualities they themselves have to offer in return.

<u>An excellent answer.</u>

I read that the school has an impressive alumnus who have referred to the excellent science facilities at the school. Since I'm really interested in Chemistry and Physics, I was excited to learn that recently you've put money into the Astro-physics department with the new telescope – in the future I'm hoping to become a research scientist. The other reason why I want to come here is that although I love science, I'm also really musical. I play the piano to grade 6 and the violin to grade 4 and I've also started to learnt to play the trumpet. I was really pleased to see the range of orchestras I could join as I love playing in a group as well as by myself.

This candidate immediately lets the interviewer know that they have done some independent research about the school and is able to refer to people who have previously attended the place. They have knowledge of the facilities the school has as well as the areas which have been recently funded which they then relate to their own interests. They build up their response by suggesting what profession they may like to pursue in the future, giving the impression that they are a forward-thinking individual with the drive to achieve something specific in the future. In addition, they ensure that they do not portray themselves as someone with a narrow focus. The link to their musical ability is enhanced by some facts, a reference to the grade they have achieved in two separate instruments together with the information that they have recently begun learning to play a new instrument – this again suggests that this child is excited by learning and is keen to experience all aspects of the curriculum. The last comment is valuable as it shows that this student is a team player and socially confident as well as feeling assured about their own knowledge and ability.

It's important when preparing your child for this particular question, that you focus on two things. Firstly, the school itself. What is it about the school that your child would really enjoy? Is it the architecture? They extensive playing fields? Is it because they specialise in sports, languages, IT? Have there been any recent additions to the grounds which your child would be excited about, such as the renovation of the music block, extension of the science facilities or the recent purchase of better lighting for the football pitches? Has there been recent funding into a particular aspect of the curriculum which your child would benefit from – for example the hiring of a particular sports coach or the introduction of a new subject such as Astrology or Greek. The second area to consider is what your child can give back to the school if they are accepted. Are they particularly gifted musically? If so, are they keen to join the orchestras and if so, which one are they most attracted to? Are they keen on science? If so, are they enthusiastic about the science curriculum at the school and the extra-curricular STEM clubs on offer? If they are good at sports, have they considered which teams are available at the school and how successful they currently are? Has your child achieved success in a particular arena, for example winning an art prize or a poetry competition? If so, this might be something to mention as it shows that they are talented enough to achieve success in their chosen arena and that they would benefit from attending the school as they would make the most of their time there.

What is your favourite subject and why?

The important thing for your child to remember here is that this is an opportunity to explain what interests they have. An answer such as 'I like Maths because my teacher is nice' is pointless as it tells the interviewer that the teacher is lovely but reveals nothing about the student.   Another simple mistake students make is trying to suggest that they like a whole range of subjects. The problem with an answer like this is that the child will end up either listing the subjects and not commenting on why they like them, or they will give a very vague or simple reason rather than going into any depth. The actual reason this question is asked is that the interviewer wants to learn what excites the child in front of them, which subject are they drawn to and what is it about it that makes them want to spend their own time learning more about it.

Let's see some possible answers.

A poor answer.

I like Maths the best because I find it really easy.

This candidate has indicated a single subject which they enjoy but their reasoning is short and vague. This is a poor answer because there is no depth and no passion. The interviewer is left wondering whether they actually find every aspect of Maths easy, and whether this is due to a natural disposition or if the child is happiest with a subject that has a clear 'right' and 'wrong' answer. This answer would be better if the child honed in on one aspect of the subject which interested them and then suggested what it was that they enjoyed. For example, "I like Maths best because I find it easy. I recently learnt how to do algebra which was really fun, it felt like I was cracking a code. That's why I like Maths I think, it's fun and I feel a bit like a detective!" In this answer, the child has shown the interviewer that they have a natural tendency towards identifying and understanding patterns, showing an enjoyment of a relatively difficult area of Maths and suggesting why they enjoy it. They have developed their response enough for the interviewer to recognise a true interest in the subject rather than just naming the subject they have the least difficulty with at school.

A good answer.

I love Music because I'm a very creative person. I really like writing my own pieces, I was particularly pleased with one I wrote with a Christmas theme because it was the first time I paired a trumpet with a piano support. I was happy that I was able to create the effect I wanted to, with the Christmas sound from the trumpet and the happy, quick paced tune giving a celebratory feel.

This student has concentrated on a subject from the Arts – other examples would include Art, Drama and DT. This is a good choice as their ability in Maths and English should already be evident from their performance on the entrance examinations. By naming a subject such as Music or Sport the child is showing the interviewer that they have interests outside the academic spectrum. In this case, the interest in the subject is supported by evidence that they have some ability there too, and also suggests that their attraction to the subject continues in their own time. They have given a specific example of a piece of music they have created outside school time, explaining their choice of instrument and the effect they were aiming to achieve. It is the extra information and explanation which makes this answer good as their enthusiasm comes across well.

An excellent answer.

I really enjoy the sciences as I'm interested in how the world works. I recently listened to a podcast about black holes and how they could power civilisations. A black hole is something that sucks in matter and energy but by stealing a bit of the energy as it goes in it's possible that we could have a power source which could last forever. The physics works out, its whether we could actually could build such a thing – it's fascinating to think about what is actually possible.

In this answer the candidate has named one subject and immediately offered an explanation as to why this is of interest to them. Their subsequent comments serve to show that their enthusiasm is deep and that they are developing their knowledge and understanding outside of school hours. In this instance, they make a reference to a podcast and are confidently able to summarise the content which indicates their high level of understanding of quite complex material. They give a quick definition of a black hole before moving on to the more theoretical aspect of the podcast but still speaking assuredly, with a confidence in what they are saying. The final comment shows their own, personal interest in the topic under discussion and shows a level of enthusiasm which seems genuine. This is a candidate with a real interest in this particular subject which they are nurturing and developing themselves.

The best way to prepare for this type of question is initially to hone in on what subject interests your child the most. After this has been established, they need to think about what aspect they enjoy the most. For example, if they say they enjoy Literacy the most, is it because they enjoy planning stories? Is it the choosing of words for the most impact on the reader? Have they entered poetry competitions with work completed outside of school? Similarly, if they enjoy Sports the most, they need to develop their answer to give more detail. Are they part of a sports team outside of school hours? Have they been chosen to captain the team because of their excellent team building skills? Were they made 'man of the match' recently, and if so, what was it that they did in that match to warrant the accolade? The most important element is to ensure that your child is answering honestly and having given it some thought. They need to think of their own experience, not name a subject because they think it will sound more impressive but really consider what subject they look forward to on their timetable and the reasons underpinning that.

How would you contribute to the extra-curricular programme?

This is a chance to show what your child will be able to give back to the school. If they are talented in a particular area, they will be expected to want to take part in whatever provision is on offer to extend pupils in this area at the school. Your child should be interested enough in the school to know what their extra-curricular provision is and to have considered what they want to take part in. Their answers will give an idea of what kind of person they are and how broad a range of interests they have.

A poor answer.

I don't really do anything outside of school. Maybe I'd join one of the sports clubs.

This student has clearly told the interviewer that they have a limited range of interests. The impression they give here is that their life outside of school hours is probably limited to playing computer games or watching television. They have also mentioned a generic 'sport' in their answer – which sport do they enjoy? The interviewer might be asking themselves whether the child has even seen the list of sports clubs and activities that are on offer at their school. A better answer might have been to indicate at least something they are doing even if it is not to do with school itself. For example, "I don't really take part in clubs or activities outside school hours because I go to our allotment after school most days. I love gardening and I'm experimenting with growing asparagus at the moment – it's quite complicated because the lant needs special conditions, but I'm excited to give it a go." In this instance, the pupil has said that they are not taking part in any activities linked to school but have supplemented their answer with information about their hobby. They are knowledgeable and articulate, giving an example of how they are extending their learning by attempting to grow more difficult produce. Although they are not availing themselves of the opportunities offered by their school their answer shows that they have interests which they are developing and suggests that they are not limited in their activities.

<u>A good answer.</u>

At the moment I go to cross-country running club bat my school every Monday and to Latin Club on a Wednesday – that's where we learn about the Romans and their culture. I read on your website that you have a few different language clubs which I'd be interested in joining and I'd probably try out the Athletics Club as well as the Running Club because I know I like running and am good at it but I'd like to see if there are other athletic events that I would enjoy.

This is a good answer because the child shows a clear knowledge of the extra-curricular clubs that the new school offer. They begin by reflecting on what clubs they are attending at their current school, giving an indication of a wider range of interests since they include an academic club (languages) and a sporting club (running). They have then linked their current interests to the provision at the new school but have not limited themselves to merely replicating the clubs they attend at the moment. Instead, they have used this as a springboard from which they will explore further options. Therefore, their current attendance at the Latin Club will be extended to other opportunities at the new establishment – no language has been eliminated from their possible list and in fact the show an interest in trying out other languages such as Italian, suggesting a real attraction to other languages as a genre rather than limiting themselves to one particular language that they may have studied at school or been familiar with via family. A similar structure applies to the way they have thought about the sports club they currently attend – the running club – since this has opened up their eyes to the extra-curricular clubs that they may attend at the new school rather than limiting them to only looking for a similar activity. This suggests a confident individual who is looking to extend themselves, someone who enjoys a challenge and isn't afraid to try out new options. They also reveal themselves to be both sporty and academic, a well-rounded individual who enjoys a mental and physical challenge.

An excellent answer.

I really enjoy going to Computer Club at my school because we learn so much about all the technology available and how it could be used in the future. I saw that you have a Year 7 Coding Club which looks really interesting and also the junior jazz orchestra which I'd like to join because I play the trumpet and love making music in a group.

This student refers first to a club they attend at their current school, together with an explanation of why they enjoy it. This then extends to their stated interest in a related club offered at their potential new school, the Coding Club. This shows that they have taken a proper look at the options available to Year 7 and that they have identified a club they feel would be a good fit for them. In addition, they indicate another hobby, a musical interest. This suggests that they are a well-rounded individual both academically and with further, non-academic pursuits. They state that they 'love making music in a group' indicating a more outgoing nature and certainly not a solitary one, giving the impression that they are socially confident and that they are equally happy working independently and with a team of people. The overall impression given in this answer is that the child is confident, with a range of outside interests and one who enjoys being with others as well as extending their own personal interests further.

Generally, when preparing for this question, your child should be familiar with the extra-curricular options available at their target school for incoming Year 7 pupils. They should relate them to their own strengths and consider which one or two clubs they would like to join with a clear, articulated response which indicates why they want to join them. A positive answer will give a strong impression of the pupil, suggesting a child with a varied set of interests who is keen to extend them further.

What career do you hope to follow in the future?

The worst response to this question would be 'I haven't thought about it'. Ideally the answer will be ambitious although realistic, with a considered career pathway in mind. Your child doesn't have to be specific about their job prospects but a recognition of their strengths and related careers would be useful. For example, if they enjoy writing stories, they may be aware that in addition to becoming a writer that they might also become a journalist, teacher or solicitor. A child with a strong interest in cricket might be interested in becoming a cricketer themselves but also express an awareness of other related careers such as a sports masseur or stadium manager. A pupil with an interest in the sciences may have thought about engineering, medicine or bio-mechanics. The important thing is that the student is articulate, confident and considered in their answer, having thought about the area they are most drawn to and the opportunities they might explore further.

Here are some example responses.

A poor answer.

My dad is an accountant and I'm really good at Maths myself so I think I will probably go into that line of work myself.

This child gives the impression that they are following in the footsteps of a loved parent but that they haven't considered their own strengths and weaknesses. It is fine to say that they have been inspired by the profession a parent is already involved in, but they need to explain what it is that attracts them to follow into it themselves. The above pupil could have extended their answer to provide some more detail of their attraction to accountancy. For example, continuing on to say "I know accountants have to pay attention to detail and they are involved in quite difficult mathematical decisions. I'm the kind of person who focuses on making sure everything is correct and that every aspect is covered and I really enjoy challenges – it's good to wrap my brain around more difficult concepts. That's why accountancy could be a really good fit for me." This extension to the original answer enables the interviewer to see that the child is aware of some of the requirements for the profession they have expressed an interest in.

<u>A good answer.</u>

I'd like to be an astronaut. They've got a really good programme in America and lots of funding for that type of work so I may end up moving there in the future. It's an exciting career because there's so much more to learn about space and we're just at the start of discovering more about it.

This student states clearly their intended career. It doesn't matter that it is ambitious or comes across as potentially unrealistic, the important thing is that they have thought about what they would like to do in the future and how that could be achieved. The sentence following their bold statement fleshes out their thinking more, indicating that they have spent time looking at the opportunities in this country and others. They have ana awareness of what work is available in America and that this is made possible by the money pumped in. This student is confident, not afraid of change and actively looking at what they might do in the future. They are not limited by physical boundaries and are happy to take their chances abroad. The last part of their answer shows some of their enthusiasm for space exploration and an understanding that there is much more to learn. They indicate an excitement for discovering more about this vast unknown entity and are stimulated by the new theories and developments under way.

<u>An excellent answer.</u>

I've really enjoyed learning about the Tudors at school recently and after that I started watching documentaries and listening to podcasts about archaeology. My parents took me to see the Mary Rose in Portsmouth so I could learn more about what they learnt about the men aboard and I'm thinking about following my interest in History further to possibly becoming an archaeologist myself. I'm also thinking about looking further into careers to do with science as well as I really enjoy Physics and I find engineering really attractive – there was a programme on tv I watched recently about different types of bridges which was great.

This is an excellent answer because the child begins by focusing on a particular subject that interests them currently – specifically stating a topic at school that has sparked an interest. They have then followed this up independently, watching relevant tv shows and listening to pertinent podcasts. This shows a thirst for knowledge and a person who will pursue a topic in their own time and under their own steam. The fact that their parents have listened to their enthusiasm and facilitated a trip to the Mary Rose indicates a supportive family life where the child is nurtured and likely to research their full academic potential as they have such a strong support behind them. Another good point about this answer is that the pupil is not limiting their future career options at a young age but simply exploring what catches their attention. Again, this suggests a student who is confident and happy to follow whatever path feels right for them. This child, in addition to the history topics, also expresses an interest in a completely different direction, having a strong liking of Physics lessons at school. As before, their further comments indicate a personality which is not limited purely to school learning but a desire to continue their education themselves. This wish to learn more and the ability to search out relevant content shows a child who is skilled at research and already able to learn independently.

In terms of preparing your child for a question about their plans for their future, you would be best to concentrate on the starting point of what topics they enjoy at school and what they like to spend their time doing at home. What have they chosen to spend their time doing? The majority of children will search out tv programmes which will reveal their leanings, or their choice of book from the library or podcast to listen to etc. This forms part of a natural conversation about future career choices. They are not looking to decide on a career at such a young age but a considered knowledge of the options available and a realisation of their own inclinations would be very beneficial. Ultimately, this question is designed to elicit a response from the student that suggests a mature consideration of their future further than simply passing an exam to gain entrance to their particular school. A well-considered answer will create a positive impression of a pupil who has looked at their own ability and inclinations and has thought themselves about their own future. A child who has something to aim for is one who will be working as hard as they can to fulfil an ambition they have identified themselves and one who is more willing to put in the effort to have it come to fruition. This is a popular question which is often asked and it gives the child a chance to talk about their dreams and desires. Let them aim high!

What books are you currently reading outside of school?

The worst answer to this question would be 'I don't like reading' or 'I only read at school'. There are some pupils who do not read voraciously but it is unlikely that they do not like to read at all. Non-fiction counts here as well as fiction, graphic novels are also fine to mention as long as they are not the comic books but well-regarded novels. For example, a re-telling of a classic book would be well received. Some students who are not drawn to fiction may spend their time reading biographies or 'how to' guides, each of these would be suitable for discussion. The other important point is that the interviewer will almost certainly be well read themselves and therefore it is a mistake for the child to state that they enjoy reading a book which they have not actually picked up. The interviewer is likely to follow up with questions about what characters they like, queries about the plot line, the ending, their opinion on an issue raised within the text. If the child has not actually read the book, they will be found out very quickly.

A poor answer.

I like reading books by Michael Morpurgo. My mum bought a set of the whole series and I'm working my way through them.

You may look at this answer and think it is in the wrong category. However, there are a number of reasons why this could be judged to be a weak reply. Firstly, the fact that mum has bought the books. The child has not made the effort themselves to get hold of books by this author or found them in the school library. It comes across as if the parent has been thinking of how they can enthuse their child about the joys of reading and has chosen a popular author to try and tempt the student to read. This assumption is further supported by the fact that the pupil says they are 'working their way through' the series. A child who is excited about reading would also become motivated to read the author's other books but there would also be comments about which author they remind them of, maybe a chat about the themes that Morpurgo covers, certainly an extension of the answer above. The other issue is that they have named an author who is very well known and prolific, aiming their books at children in the 10 – 14 year age range. Ideally, your child would name some more challenging titles and authors, showing that they have an above average reading age, an active interest in reading and an ability to engage with more difficult texts.

<u>A good answer.</u>

I enjoy reading books by David Walliams. My favourite is 'Billionaire Boy' because it made me think about what I would do if I had lots of money. I like David Walliams' books because he takes ordinary people as the main characters. I feel like I can relate to them, even the female ones like the girl in 'Mr Stink'! At the moment thought I'm reading 'Robinson Crusoe' because my friend said he thought I would like it. So far, I'm enjoying it.

The first author named is again one who is popular with a young audience, typically age 8 and above. The reason this is a better response is that the child has extended their answer without prompting to indicate which is their favourite text (showing that they have read a good number of them already – they refer to two by name – this conveys the impression that they have not just read one from the collection but that they are genuinely interested in reading) and giving a reason behind their choice. The second author named is a recommendation from a friend. This lets the interviewer know that the child is happy to talk about reading with their friends and that they are living in a positive reading culture where reading is valued and seen as positive. The text named is relatively challenging and this indicates a strong reading level. As the child says they are 'enjoying it' (the text) they must have an understanding of the plot despite the complexity of the vocabulary. This therefore gives a favourable impression of the child and their level of comprehension.

<u>An excellent answer.</u>

I recently read 'Treasure Island' which I really enjoyed because of the action. I liked 'The Wolves of Willoughby Chase' for a similar reason, the writing was so pacy and the storyline built up to the climax – I stayed up to finish the book because it was so exciting! The best part was when the wolves attacked the train. Right now, I'm reading 'Call of the Wild' which is quite action packed too. I'm up to the part where Buck gets dognapped.

All three of the books named are challenging in nature but the child refers to them naturally as part of their everyday reading suggesting a strong level of comprehension and a positive engagement with the written word. They have linked the texts together well in their response, comparing their level of action. This is a higher skill which is quite complex – the fact that this student is comfortable using it is very positive. They have referred to the texts in some detail, for example mentioning the part they found most exciting in 'The Wolves of Willoughby Chase'. This lets the interviewer know that the student really has read the text and isn't just name dropping, they have a working knowledge of the plot and how it has been constructed to engage the reader. This student is clearly attracted to action packed novels since all three have this in common, revealing something of their personality to the interviewer. The confidence they display when discussing the texts and enthusiasm for the ones they mention conveys their own passion for reading and suggests a student who is engaged with the written word. If they are able to read this type of book the assumption that follows is that they are likely to be strong at expressing themselves on paper too because their reading will be continually informing their vocabulary and they will be picking up examples of structure and plot all the time. They are likely to have a good grasp on the use of punctuation to enhance the mood and atmosphere of their own creative writing too.

When considering your own child's reading habits, you can help prepare them for this type of question by broadening their reading horizons. Introduce them to classic literature, read with them, ask them what they think about the issues raised, find the films of the books to watch with them after they have enjoyed the book first. Another benefit to becoming familiar with these older, more challenging texts, is that there is a propensity for schools to use extracts from these older texts for the comprehension section of the entrance exam itself. There are two reasons for this – firstly the vocabulary is generally considered to be more challenging and it offers more opportunities for the examiners to see which child has the decoding skills to understand the text even though it is initially hard to read and secondly, the copyright is free due to the age of the text. Therefore, it is important to encourage your child to read these classic children's books since extracts from them are more likely to come up in the exam. Ultimately though, you are aiming to create a reading culture in your own home and helping your child to discover authors and genres. This can be achieved through a myriad of ways. Membership of the library and regular trips there; showing a positive attitude to reading at home – if your child sees you taking the time to read then they will be far more likely to view it as a valuable and pleasurable activity that they will spend time on themselves as well; making the most of book sales and having a variety of books always available at home. If you have a more reluctant reader, present reading in a different way. Share a newspaper with them and discuss the stories and issues covered. Introduce them to audio books and non-fiction titles. It may take some trial and error to discover what your own child will respond to best but it is worth making the effort when you consider all the benefits reading can bestow.

Tell me more about what you do outside of school.

This question is designed to establish how your child spends their time outside if the school gates. A very poor answer would be where the child mentions computer games and television. Both are perfectly satisfactory ways of relaxing but in this instance the interviewer is hoping to learn more about the student as a person and what they can offer for their school. This is an opportunity to describe participation in sports clubs, competitions entered (and won), playing an instrument etc. Ideally the candidate will be able to shine a light on their interests and hobbies away from the academic focus. Therefore, they may refer to spending time on the computer but maybe learning how to code – they may be proud of coding a particular game for example. This is different to being the player of a computer game as it uses a completely different and more admirable skill set. With regard to television. It would be preferable for the child to refer to one or two specific programmes which may have led to an interest in this field and one they have subsequently taken further. For example, watching 'Springwatch' and then taking part in the garden watch research which the presenters encouraged viewers to try. The student may then move on to discuss the variety of birds which had visited their garden and their own making of a bird feeder or an interest in when and where the birds disappear to at different points of the year. The main point is that the viewing of television or the interest in computers can come across in a positive light if the impact on the child is conveyed effectively during their interview.

A poor answer.

My mum takes me to football once a week and I also practise my skills in the garden at home – I can do 34 knee bounces now! The record is 196 which is the goal I'm aiming to beat.

The initial focus is on the parent facilitating the child's out of school focus. However, this answer is strengthened when they build on their answer, relating how they are inspired to improve their skills by working on them independently at home. It sounds like the student is rather single minded, targeting only one skill rather than suggesting a more rounded approach. They also cite the example of someone who holds the record for the highest number of knee bounces performed in one go. Although this is an admirable feat, it does not necessarily translate into a better player on the football pitch. Ideally, the child wants to convey their enthusiasm and commitment to improving while also ensuring they come across as a team player. They may cite references to footballers they admire and comment on what particular reason they have for their reverence – this would show their knowledge of the wider sport and suggest aspects they admire and hope to develop themselves. This could become a great answer if considered carefully and developed so the student presents themselves in the best possible light.

A good answer.

I spend a lot of time outside at our allotment – I've just finished turning over the soil ready for planting our next crop. I did some research online and asked some of the other gardeners, and I've decided to…

The first thing to notice about this answer is that the child clearly enjoys being outside. They are not a single-minded, academic individual, they are able to commit themselves to a pursuit which is physical. However, alongside that, they have made it clear that they have ownership of the project. They do not refer to what the family have decided to grow, or given the impression that their parents have made the decisions and they are following instructions – the use of the pronoun 'I' indicates the pride in their personal decision making. More impressively, they have not made a quick, off the cuff choice, they make it clear that they have been researching options on the internet and also liaising with other allotment owners. This indicates an ability to use research tools online and a personality where the child is confident enough to talk to other adults who they are not related to. Both of these attributes are very positive – the so-called 'soft skills' of being able to communicate effectively and with confidence and the more well-known skills of being able to research and discover an answer by themselves, utilising the search engines to come to a reasonable conclusion. This answer also opens up the discussion with the interviewer well, they have a number of options in terms of leading the conversation forward. They could move on to discuss the choice the child made in terms of growing vegetables and look more deeply into their decision-making skills. Alternately, they may choose to talk about their pride in their hobby and lead them to expand further on what they feel they benefit from. Generally, this is an answer which indicates a child who has a confidence and happiness in their life outside of school.

An excellent answer.

I enjoy exploring different artists and techniques. I entered a local competition where they asked us to design a poster celebrating the town and I won second place! I used block colours and worked my way up from a pencil design…

In this answer the child begins by suggesting a broad interest in art although they indicate a personal desire to discover more. They are aware that specific artists are linked to different genres and artistic techniques and are excited about their discoveries. This is a child who has decided to research further out of a personal interest, a child who has been inspired by seeing the work of a variety of artists and is able to distinguish between them easily. They move on to discuss a competition which they have entered and achieved a commendable second place. This is a great achievement and one they are rightly proud of. Occasionally parents feel that their child can only mention the competitions they have taken part in if they have won but it is worth mentioning even if they do not come in the top winners – what is important is that the student has developed their own skills and is proud of their work. In this instance, the student moves on to refer to a particular technique they have been inspired to use following their research into the work of other artists. They are confident in describing the process they have followed and excited about the result. The enthusiasm and personal nature of the response is what makes this answer so good.

When faced with a question of this nature, the best answers encourage further discussion. They shine a light on the interest of the child and show how they choose to spend their own time and what they consider to be the best way to spend their energy and effort. It is important that the pupil shows themselves in the best possible light, which is why they should spend some time considering their response to this question. Although they may enjoy spending a lot of their time crafting for example, could they expand on their reply and thus enthuse the interviewer as well? For example, if they refer to spending their time practising the piano, they may wish to add some information about how long they have been learning and what level they have achieved. Maybe refer to composers they admire or even mention compositions they themselves have endeavoured to create. If they refer to spending time with their friends, especially enjoying trips to the local farm park, the answer could be strengthened by sharing an anecdote about how they helped a friend who was in difficulty on one of the activity pieces, or discussing how they have learnt about one particular animal who caught their attention. It is in the extra detail that the interviewer will glean what type of chid they have in front of them. Is this candidate one who is keen and eager to learn more about the world around them? Are they inspired by the works of other individuals? Have they developed a set of skills independently? These are the questions an interviewer is sifting through as they engage in conversation with your child, seeing what excited them, what they are keen to share and how well they can communicate their passions.

What would you say are your strengths and weaknesses?

This is a classic interview question which many adults are faced with. There are two parts to the answer. The worst answer would be if the pupil sat and could not come up with an answer for either identifying an area of strength of an area which they considered to be weak. A similarly poor answer would be where the child listed of four or five general areas they felt they were very strong (For example, "I'm really good at Maths, Science, PE and Spelling") but being unable to name any area they felt they were not as capable. The best answers will be more specific with the child naming one or two areas they feel they are strong (and ideally not just naming a subject but an area within them) and similarly mentioning an area they know is weak combined with an understanding of how they hope to become better at it.

A poor answer.

I'm good at Maths and Science but find English really hard.

This is a poor response because of the very vague, all encompassing answer. Is the child genuinely very good at all aspects of Maths and Science? Isn't there one area in particular where they shine especially well? In a similar vein, they seem to have labelled themselves as being weak at every aspect of English. Are they referring to spelling? Punctuation? Planning stories? Getting ideas? It is unlikely that a student is genuinely poor at one particular subject in its entirety. This suggests a child who has a negative self-image and has decided at a very young age what subjects they are able to do well and which they are unable to access to a strong degree. An interviewer is looking for children with a high sense of self-worth coupled with a degree of self-awareness – hence the ability to identify areas they may enjoy or have experienced a high element of success, alongside an ability to point to a certain element they know they struggle with. However, these areas would usually be more specific and certainly naming an entire subject as being an area of weakness is a sad comment on the child's perception of themselves.

<u>A good answer.</u>

I'm strong at Maths, especially Algebra. I've always been able to see patterns and algebra seems a bit like that to me – it's like solving puzzles and I enjoy that. I'm weaker at planning essays because a lot of the time I'd rather just get on with writing my story! I do understand what my teacher is talking about though and I know that if I take the time to think about the plan before I start writing my story tends to be better structured.

This candidate has highlighted a subject area they feel they are strong at and immediately zoomed in on a specific area within this subject. They have then explained what it is about algebra that they enjoy (I've always been able to see patterns… it's like solving puzzles and I enjoy that) and suggested this could be the reason for their strength in this area. When relating their weakness, they mention a specific area – planning essays. The reason that this answer is classified as 'good' is that they indicate straight away the fact that they know what they can do to improve. This child is not helpless or passively accepting limitations. Instead, they have looked at the area of weakness, identified why it is so, and suggested how they could improve as a result. This answer is a big step up from the previous example simply because of the detail given and the ability of the student to suggest how they themselves will move themselves out of the 'weak' category. Interestingly, they are also able to state that when they put the action into place (planning ahead of writing) they can see a distinct improvement in a measurable aspect of their writing – the "story tends to be better structured". If you were to ask this child in five years' time the same question - to identify their strengths and weaknesses - they may have the same response for identifying their strengths. However, the identified weakness is likely to be different. This is because they are currently aware of the issue regarding planning. They recognise that their work is improved when they take the time to think about their essay before starting and they are therefore very likely to take the time to fix this issue in the near future.

<u>An excellent answer.</u>

I find it frustrating when I'm in group tasks with other pupils who aren't as quick as me, but I've learnt to make it better by encouraging them and showing them the methods I use. I'd say my strengths are my interest in Maths because my whole family enjoys numbers and calculations.

This student has identified a personal weakness which comes to the fore when working with other students, especially those who are slower. What makes this answer an excellent one is that the child has decided on a method to counteract their feelings and to make the situation more constructive both for themselves and the other children in the group. Instead of venting their frustrations, they instead 'encourage them' and 'show them the methods I use'. This more collaborative approach shows the child has made a positive change which enables them to feel useful as they are aiding another member of the group. This is a much better reaction to feeling of frustration than to sit, annoyed, waiting for the rest of the group to catch up. When discussing their strengths, this student refers to their 'interest in Maths' – a wide subject area – but then they narrow the focus down to reflect on the familial impact on their ability. They refer to their 'whole family' who enjoy 'numbers and calculations' – a comment which indicates a strong family unit who enjoy working on mathematical problems together for fun. Although the child does not say in detail what aspect of Maths they are very good at, the fact that they do not use the opportunity to boast about their numerical achievements but are happy to acknowledge the fact that other members of the family are equally strong at the subject suggests an attractive personality trait.

Ultimately, this question is designed to elicit a personal response from the child. What do they perceive themselves to be their strengths and weaknesses. Their actual ability will be measured via tests and this is therefore not being asked to see who is better at Maths and who is better at English – this will be all too clear when the tests are marked. Instead, the question offers an opportunity to discover the child's perception of themselves in relation to others. Are they a boastful type who believes they are the best at absolutely everything they try? Are they confident and happy to approach any subject with a positive mind set, able to take any initial failures and to work on them. These children are not limited by any experience – they take the positive and the negative and learn from both. The saddest situation is where a child has a very negative view of themselves – to have written off an entire subject area of a particular topic and decided that they are unable to tackle that – this is a child who lacks resilience and has not learnt that every person experiences failure. A weakness does not necessarily mean that it will remain that way for ever. Instead, children need to be able to face difficulties with courage and be happy and willing to have another go, to keep trying other methods of learning.

The interviewer is hoping to find that the candidate has a positive view of their abilities and that they are confident and pleased to be able to talk about where they shine. Similarly, they want to know that the child is not easily dissuaded from trying to learn something which is difficult, whether learning to master an instrument, read a poem out in front of a class or to complete a difficult sum. The important thing is that the pupil is willing and keen to learn from their mistakes rather than disappointed in their own ability. A candidate who has a positive, 'can-do' attitude is going to make a much better impression than one who is negative and cannot see how they can move on in a certain area. Overall, a successful candidate will answer this question with consideration and a positive spin on both their self-identified strengths and weaknesses.

If I asked your friends to describe you, what would they say?

The most important thing her is that the child thinks of positive aspects that their friends may mention about them. The easiest way to tackle this question is that they consider three appropriate adjectives which they feel other children may use to describe them and to be prepared to discuss each one in more detail in relation to how they feel about themselves. This is a question designed to discover what impression the child feels they make on others around them, their answers will reveal a degree of self-awareness and hopefully shine another light on the personality of the student which may not be revealed in any other circumstance. For example, if they say others would say they are thoughtful because they suggested making a class card for a fellow pupil who was about to spend some time in hospital. This would show a caring aspect of their personality as well as a willingness to take on a leadership role in taking the initiative in this thoughtful venture.

A poor answer.

I can't think of anything… maybe loud, bouncy and fun?

The initial response where the child cannot think of any description at all is acceptable – if the student had not expected this question, they may be trying to come up with ideas on the spot which can be difficult to do, especially under pressure and with the knowledge that the interviewer is waiting for an answer. The actual words chosen to describe themselves work together to create the suggestion that this child may come across as potentially disruptive in the classroom and one who finds it difficult to regulate themselves. Individually the adjectives could be seen in a more positive light, especially if they were followed with more of an explanation. The initial word 'loud' might be an attempt to explain that in the playground they enjoy making themselves heard and that they enjoy lively games – this would link to the second adjective 'bouncy' which in the context of a break time comes across as a far more positive attribute. The last adjective 'fun' again needs to be put in context. Do they mean they are a popular member of the class because they are able to thin of lots of games for the rest of the class to take part in when outside? Are they referring to situations in the classroom where their idea of 'fun' might not coincide with that of others – not taking an Art lesson seriously for example or blocking a toilet with paper towels for the 'fun' of seeing the reaction of other children when the bathroom becomes flooded. This is why the child ideally needs to spend a bit of time thinking about their answer and to consider truthfully how others might perceive them while also being mindful that the interviewer is looking to accept students who would be a good addition to the year group.

A good answer.

I think my classmates would describe me as happy, friendly and good at Maths. Sometimes I help other people with bits of Maths they find tricky so they might say I'm helpful and caring too.

In this instance the child has thought of some attributes that suggest a well-rounded individual. There is not a lot of detail included in their response, but the interviewer has aspects they can pick up on if they wish to delve deeper. The first two adjectives, 'happy' and 'friendly', are traits which any teacher would wish to find amongst their pupils. A cheerful child who enjoys school and wants to spend their time their learning the classroom and enjoying the company of their classmates is a wonderful thing. The fact that they say others would describe them as 'friendly' suggests an inclusive nature where they are welcoming of other students and certainly not part of a clique or someone who might enjoy ostracising other pupils at any point. The last part of their answer where they state that their friends might describe them as 'good at Maths' is subjective but reveals that within their own, limited classroom setting they are viewed by others as strong in this particular subject. The follow up information is interesting because they continue on to say that they 'help other people with bits of Maths they find tricky' – this shows that they do not get frustrated or angry with the limitations of other children in the classroom when tackling the subject, but they are willing to share their own knowledge and understanding. This also indicates a child who genuinely is able and possibly gifted at Maths since the ability to explain to others how to approach a problem is linked to a stronger understanding themselves of the issue they are grappling with. It is nearly impossible to explain something to someone else unless you have a clear understanding yourself. Of course, this child may be referring to the fact that they are happy to share the answers to Maths problems with other children rather than their explanations – a skilled interviewer would soon discover which was the case!

An excellent answer.

I think my friends would describe me as approachable, honest and they'd probably say that I love Maths!

At first glance this answer may seem to be very similar to the previous, good, response. However, the adjectives chosen this time are more nuanced and certainly not as vague as the previous candidate. Rather than describe themselves as 'happy' and 'friendly' they have said they are 'approachable' and 'honest'. The first adjective implies that they are a friendly and welcoming person, one who a student new to a class might be buddied up with. The second word chosen, 'honest', shows us that the child believes they are regarded as having a strong moral code and can be relied on to tell the truth in different situations. The last comment says that they think their friends would say that they 'love Maths'. This contrasts with the previous candidate who said that their friends might say that they are 'great at Maths'. The difference between the two responses is that the first one suggests an external point of view based on results and status in the classroom. The second observation with the choice of the verb 'loves' indicates a more personal connection with the subject Maths. This second candidate is letting the examiner know that their friends do not just recognise their ability in the subject but that they also appreciate their own joy in the subject. This candidate is more likely to be looking at Mathematical problems at home or asking for extra information from the teacher, a student who really relishes pushing themselves in this subject.

This question is one which enables an interviewer to glean so much more from the student depending on their response. The candidate has an opportunity here to give a very strong impression of themselves and a chance to put forward 'soft skills' which might not otherwise come to their attention. Other adjectives which might be worth considering are 'caring', 'cheerful' or 'creative' as long as each adjective is coupled with an explanation of why someone might use these adjectives to describe them. The most important consideration for this question is ensuring that the student discusses each comment, so the interviewer is not left in any doubt as to what the child is trying to convey about themselves. Listing two or three adjectives with no commentary leaves the answer open to misunderstanding or misinterpretation. Other responses may link to more physical abilities such as a comment about their football skills or that they are really fast in the Sports Day races. Again, this type of reply is fine if coupled with some additional information. For example, the student who says that 'my friends would describe me as really talented at football' might move on to talk about their attendance at various football clubs and trophies such as 'team player' that they have won.

Ideally, a child will indicate a couple of personality traits that will be viewed as desirable alongside a more definable attribute. The most important thing is that they present a truthful idea of how they feel they appear to other children, with an understanding of which characteristics others see as attractive.

What has been your biggest challenge?

Again, some adults may have been asked this question themselves at an interview although usually they are being asked to reflect on a challenge they have faced in a work environment. Ideally, a candidate will be able to reflect on their own lives whether at school or at home and will be able to identify a time where they had to work to overcome something. The most important aspect of this question is not the identification of the challenge but the child's response to the difficulty. A strong candidate will be able to state a specific instance and crucially will be able to discuss strategies they have put into place to address this problem. A common response and one that is not well received by interviewers is when the candidate says their biggest challenge has been 'preparing for the entrance exam' or 'getting ready for this interview'. The interview is often presented as being 'just a chat' by schools and not something that can be prepared for. This, combined with the fact that they wish to glean knowledge about the personality of the student as well as their ability in certain subjects makes any suggestion of preparation for the interview a poor answer. Similarly, if they refer to their biggest challenge as being preparation for the entrance examinations the interviewer may be left with the impression that the child may not be innately intelligent and has simply been heavily tutored for the tests. This then cast doubts on the ability of the child to hold their own at a selective school and even suggests that the child may be unsuitable for a place. Therefore, it is important for the child to think of another, unrelated, incident which they may have found difficult and that they are able to discuss what they have put in place to overcome this.

A poor answer.

I felt really upset when we lost the final football game in the local competition. I'm hoping next year we win instead.

It's good that this child acknowledges their feelings about losing an important match – when a team has been geared up to win all season and they have reached the last game there is a lot riding on it. What is more disappointing is that they have not said anything about how they have subsequently learnt to deal with their hurt feelings or the anger and frustration they may have felt at their perceived team failure. Instead, they give the impression that in future they hope to avoid this feeling and concentrate entirely on winning. This means that the student has not learnt any coping strategies or learnt how to be resilient in difficult circumstances. They are not able to celebrate the achievements of the team – coming second in a competition is a great success – and instead are still focused on their view of the situation which is a negative one.

This answer would be better if they indicated that they had learnt to embrace a growth mindset, learning from the situation and putting into place strategies which would help them to cope with the next time their team did not win. After all, it is unusual for a sports team to continuously win and therefore losing is an experience they will need to learn to deal with more effectively than they do at present.

A good answer.

I found it difficult when I moved into a new area two years ago. I left my old friends behind and it was difficult to join a brand-new school where everyone knew each other. It's worked out well though, I decided to be positive and made myself open to the idea of making new friends. I've now got my old friends from X as well as my new friends from Y – I'm really pleased that I didn't stick in the past but opened myself up to new friendships.

This student has identified a specific episode in their life where they had no control over the situation – their preference would obviously have been to stay where they were previously living but the adults had made a decision to move to a new area. They acknowledge their feelings, saying that they found the idea of moving 'difficult' but crucially they made a decision themselves not to mope and focus on the past and the friendships from before but to adopt a positive attitude to the new school. This resulted in the child making new friends while still retaining their friendships from before. As they state themselves, this situation 'worked out well' despite their initial fears and misgivings.

The important thing here is that the child did not give up in the face of this big life change. Instead, they decided to embrace the situation and to open themselves up to a new and potentially scary experience. This child has faced a challenge and overcome it, a challenge not of their making but one they have been able to turn into an advantage, making new friends to add to their older set.

An excellent answer.

I was really nervous when I needed to sit my grade 5 theory exam. I'm really good at playing the piano but my teacher explained that I needed to pass the theory test in order to access the higher grades for the practical examinations. To begin with I felt a bit reluctant but as I started to commit myself to understanding the theory, I found I learnt a lot and I was surprised to realise that it actually helped me in my own playing once I knew…

In this instance, the child makes it clear that they enjoy playing the piano and that they have reached at least grade 5 in the practical examinations. At this point, all students must pass the grade 5 theory examination to be able to progress further. Some pupils decide to begin a new instrument at this moment or even give up playing altogether. I have heard complaints about music theory being 'boring' and 'nothing to do with playing'. This student, after their initial reservations, decided to focus on the task at hand. They say that they 'started to commit' to the work and ultimately gained an understanding of why this recommendation is in place. A piano player or indeed, player of any instrument, should find a background knowledge of music theory supports their playing – the two are intertwined and one impacts on the other.

This child states that they were 'surprised to realise it actually helped me in my own playing' and they continue to explain how exactly the theory had had an effect on their playing. The reason this is an excellent answer is that the pupil has identified a specific moment when they felt they faced a big challenge – the theory examination. Instead of baulking, they make a conscious decision to step up and do their best. In addition, they also recognise the benefit of having done so – this is why this answer is excellent – the child has completed a task which initially they preferred to shy away from, feeling it completely irrelevant to them. They make the choice to embrace the task and subsequently appreciate what they have learnt and can express the impact it has had on their life.

This question is interesting firstly because it reveals what the candidate identifies as 'a challenge'. It is an open question and therefore they can choose anything they like to discuss. They may refer to a relatively small challenge, such as the time at school when they had a tricky time making a shield for a History topic. This could be a good answer if they then explain what difficulties they experienced and then, more importantly, take the time to discuss how these were surmounted. It doesn't necessarily matter what they choose to talk about in relation to this question, as long as the student makes it clear that they did not give up at the first sign of difficulty but instead decided to face the problem. Their success in dealing with the situation would be enhanced if they are able to give some further detail about what they have learnt from the encounter, whether this is something that can be measured or simply a personal sense of accomplishment or a growing sense of belief in themselves and their ability to cope under pressure.

What do you expect to be doing 10 years from now?

This is another question which comes up in interviews for adults. The interviewer is asking it because they want to gauge how much interest the student has in their future. It is not asking them about a long time away – the classic 'what do you want to be when you grow up? – rather, it is looking at a shorter viewpoint. Of course, their answers will reveal whether the child has put any consideration into what they want to do work wise in the future, but they will also show whether a child has any idea about how that career path might be achieved. In addition, the student might suggest something completely different which again reveals something about their interests and their outlook. For example, they may suggest that in ten years' time they would like to be living in another country or working on a farm. They may hope to be married with children or to have seven dogs living with them. Whatever they speak about will show the interviewer the kind of person they are and will give an idea of their aspirations. The worst answer a student can give to the question is 'I don't know' because it suggests that the candidate has no interest in the future and that they are only focused on the present. Ideally, a child will have something to aim for, even at this young age. An understanding of what interests them and what they want to study further, an idea of where they might like to live, what they would like to be doing for a career. A pupil who has not considered anything further than their own schooling would give a relatively poor impression.

A poor answer.

Mum and Dad both work at X hospital so I'll probably do the same thing.

There is nothing wrong with a child being inspired by their parents – in fact it is admirable. The trouble here is that this child appears to have put no thought into their own future. They seem to assume that they are automatically going to follow the same career path simply because both parents have already become members of the medical profession. It would be more commendable if the child mentioned that their parents worked at X hospital and that they had asked them about their jobs, piquing their own interest in various options within the medical field. By generically stating that they will dimply 'work at X hospital', this child alludes to a lack of knowledge about the specific jobs their parents actually do, the emphasis is on their place of work rather than their actual professions.

A good answer.

I love Science so I expect I would have decided to go to university to study something like that. I've really enjoyed looking at electrical circuits at school and I think that might be something I'd be interested in following up later.

This child has given an idea of which subject they enjoy at school but have not limited themselves to simply saying that they hope to study this at university or to be in a job relating to that. Instead, they mention something specific they have enjoyed within the topic itself – a similar response might be a child who says that they would like to become a novelist because they enjoy the creative writing aspect of English lessons or a student who says they hope they are taking part in archaeological digs because they have had a good time learning about the discovery of the tombs of Egypt during History lessons. In each example, the pupil has not stuck to one vague subject title. They have not said 'I hope to be focussing on the Sciences' or 'I expect I'll be an accountant because I'm good at Maths' – these responses are more nuanced that that. These pupils are able to look into what aspect of the subject or topic has interested them and they subsequently look at how they might decide to develop this interest further when they are older.

An excellent answer.

I'd like to have finished my time at this school having taken advantage of all it has to offer – especially the Science labs as they look great after the refurbishment last year. I'd like to aim for Cambridge or Oxford although I'm not sure what I'd want to specialise in.

This candidate begins with some commentary on the current situation – they are taking part in an interview to attend a selective school. They allude to the fact that they hope to have been accepted and move on to refer to the school specifically. There is a comment about the refurbishment of the Science labs which took place 'last year'. This shows that the child is aware of this school in particular – they may be attending interviews for a number of schools but in response to this question they have indicated their desire to attend this one in particular and shown that they are interested enough to take note of what the school has spent money on in recent years. Another child might refer to the excellent reputation the school has for music and refer to their own musical ability or talk about the swimming pool and their hope to take join the swimming team in addition to the club sessions they attend in their own time, with a goal of entering some prestigious competitions further down the line.

In this instance, the child moves on after their comment about the recent refurbishment to name two universities they hope to apply for in the future. These are the best-known educational establishments in England, and by mentioning them the child is indicating their belief in their academic prowess and their awareness of the existence of these places. This candidate has an idea of what they want to be doing in the future – they haven't mentioned anything specifically about which subject they may wish to specialise in, but there is an assumption that they will work hard and achieve well academically, opening the door for the chance to attend one of these revered institutions.

The most impressive answers from candidates will reveal a child who has some idea of their future. This needn't be specific but should be clearly led by the student and coming from a personal perspective. There may be some parental influence apparent – the child who named Oxford and Cambridge is unlikely to have come across them by chance. This therefore indicates a household where such institutions are referred to as being places a child can aspire to attend. An important trait that the interviewer is looking for is a household who are invested in education themselves. A number of families see private education as an opportunity to allow their children to be educated outside of the home – they may be said to 'divorce' themselves from the education of their off-spring, seeing it as outsourcing. It is far more attractive to have a family who are interested in supporting the school as they take the child on their educational journey. Thus, the child who knows what university is and has some awareness of their purpose indicates that they are part of a family who value education and have strong desires for their children, not just to attend a certain school and leave them to make their own way but who are fully behind their child, involving themselves in their progress and interested in what contribution they might make in addition to the opportunities provided by the school.

The most important element in terms of answering this question is that the child is confident in their own future – they feel like they have ownership of their destiny and are interested in their own time ahead. They are not limited to simply looking at which school they might attend but have been encouraged to consider further along the line than that and are excited about the opportunities the future may hold for them. This can only come from the parents playing an active role in the child's life, talking to them about the chances they may have later in life and giving them an idea of how to navigate the exciting future ahead of them.

Who do you admire and why?

Hopefully the candidate will not have to think too deeply to suggest a person who they admire and look up to. Again, it isn't necessarily the actual person they choose but more their explanation of why that is the person they admire. Answers could range from fictional characters such as Atticus Finch from the book To Kill and Mockingbird to a family member or a person who died a long time ago. It might be a well-known public figure or a complete unknown. The actual choice is irrelevant and not what the interviewer is concentrated on. They are listening for the second stage of the question – the why. If the explanation is vague then the child will leave a poor impression, giving the idea that they have said they admire the person named simply because they have heard other people mention them and they feel they should do the same – they may name a note-worthy person for example without knowledge or understanding of what it is they are respected for. A good impression will be given if the pupil is keen to reveal what it is they themselves admire about the named person, conveying their admiration easily to the interviewer.

A poor answer.

Maybe GamerGirl – they're an influencer I like to look at. Or maybe Kim Kardashian because she's really well-known. People are interested in her because she changes her look all the time and she's always in the papers and magazines.

This candidate has named two people who they say they admire, both coming from the media. Gamergirl is described as an 'influencer' and the child says that they like to look at their content. They do not reveal to the interviewer what it is in particular about this person that they admire but it is likely to be simply the fact that they are popular on social media. Similarly, they name Kim Kardashian as the second person they admire. This time, they follow up with an idea as to why they are popular, hinting at what they feel is an admirable quality. They state that 'people are interested in her because she changes her look all the time'. This is a rather shallow reason to admire someone – it may be that the child is swayed by the fact that the Kardashians are 'always in the papers and magazines' and this is what they equate with success. Admiring a person for their looks or their presence on tv or in social media is a relatively poor response because this indicates that this is what the child aspires to emulate in the future. If they believe success is measured by likes from strangers or linked to physical appearance, they are missing out on understanding what are truly admirable qualities. There is an emphasis here on the outward look of a person rather than their contribution to the world.

This candidate may be seen in a negative light because they are showing their interest in superficial appearances and aspects of life such as social media presence which are far removed from the goals of an educational establishment. This answer might be salvaged if the child expressed a knowledge of and admiration for Kim Kardashian's charitable endeavours. Mention of her donation of $1 million to the Armenia Fund or the fact that she donates her clothes to the Dream Foundation would show that the child has chosen to name this person as someone to admire not because of how they look but because of something they have done to make the world a better place, something worthy of admiration. Mentioning someone simply because they have become well-known by being in a television show or making content on social media is not as impressive.

A good answer.

I would say that I admire my dad. He came to this country when he was a teenager with his family, and he's worked really hard to get the job he has now. I think other people admire him as well because they sometimes ask him to help with different jobs – I heard one of his friends asking for his advice the other day.

This child indicates a high level of respect and admiration for their father. They expand on their answer, giving more insight into the reasons behind their choice to name their dad as the person they most admire. To begin with, they recognise the challenges their father faced when arriving in a new country as a teenager. It is a difficult time in anyone's life but to face such an upheaval at this delicate age would be even more challenging. Instead of buckling under the stress of the situation, the father chose to make the most of the opportunities they saw around them. Their child states that their dad has 'worked really hard' to achieve their goal. It seems likely that the child will have inherited this strong work ethic since they admire it in someone so close to them. The child sees a correlation between 'working really hard' and being able to 'get the job', suggesting that they have learnt from their father at a young age to identify a goal and to work towards this identified, end result. Furthermore, this child has heard other adults asking their dad for 'help' and 'advice'. The fact that grown-ups are choosing to approach this child's father for their opinion has had an impact on their view. If adults seek out and listen to their dad's advice, it seems logical that they too will listen to their father and take note of what they say. This indicates a child who is coming from a strong family unit where there is an emphasis on endeavour and achievement. This is the kind of attitude that is very attractive in prospective students and this child would come across in a very positive light.

<u>An excellent answer.</u>

I admire Steve Jobs because he showed such leadership skills in the workplace. He was central to the development of computers and smartphones and at the forefront of establishing the way we use computer systems all over the world. I admire his clear vision and inner drive to make that happen.

This child has chosen a well-known public figure to name as the person they admire the most. The important thing here is the reasoning behind their choice. Firstly, they allude to Jobs' leadership skills. This couples with their later comments about his 'clear vision and inner drive', qualities which meant he was able to move forward, taking others with him. He was able to share his vision for the future and made others excited about the prospects he foresaw. This child not only recognises the achievements of the man, the fact that he led the development of computers and smartphones from very early on but also points to Jobs' ability to lead a team forward very successfully. In fact, it is this quality, above the actual achievements of the man (which they clearly know) that they state is the reason for his admiration. If this student can perceive and appreciate these qualities in Steve Jobs then they are likely to try and emulate them themselves. This would result in a student who is excited about developing these intrinsic skills – the ability to lead a team effectively, sharing a vision and making it happen rather than simply listing off his achievements.

This question can deliver some real insights into the mindset of the candidate. The person they state they admire will reveal what values they believe are important themselves. Whether these relate to the appearance of the person, their achievements, personality or skills they display. When preparing to answer this question, the pupil should take some time to decide on who they admire and think about the impression they are trying to give of themselves. For example, if they say that they admire Harry Kane for his footballing ability, this shows where the child's interests lie. It is not as useful as an answer which may pay tribute to a person's achievements but puts them in the context of that individual's personality and the hard work they have had to put in to reach their goals. If the student in the example above continued on to explain that they admired Harry Kane for his dedication and determination the interviewer may receive the impression that the child not only sees that the footballer is talented, but that they have had to work to nurture that talent. The interviewer may conclude that since the student understands the value of hard work and practice, that they themselves are likely to put that into place for themselves.

What makes you unique?

This is a fantastic, open question where the student can take the opportunity to explain what makes them stand out from the crowd of other students being interviewed for a place at the school. A very poor response would be a child who said they don't like to stand out or be different, that they want to be just like everybody else. A response of this nature indicates a child with low self-esteem and likely to be low in confidence. The ability to praise oneself for an exceptional ability is not necessarily linked to an outgoing nature or a question to indicate whether the student is an introvert or an extrovert. It is a chance for the interviewer to learn something new about the candidate and for them to suggest why they are a fantastic choice for entry to the school.

A poor answer.

I'm really good at the piano and the guitar. A lot of people only take up one instrument, but I decided to take up two.

This answer is only poor because although the child may be unique among their friends or class at school for playing two instruments, many candidates for selective schools play two or even three. A lot of candidates can play to a very high standard, with children achieving grades 6 and above relatively common. This answer could be improved by making it more personal. They could still mention their musical abilities but focus more on their approach to practice sessions or their inclination towards a particular musical style which they perceive to be less popular but nevertheless one they enjoy and admire the musicians within the genre. For example, they may say they enjoy playing the piano and guitar and the unique aspect of their practice is that they really enjoy folk music. Maybe they have researched some of the older folk tales from other countries which have been set to music. Another possibility would be if they still mentioned their musical capabilities to the interviewer, then building up to the 'unique' aspect. They may talk about their musical tastes which they feel are unique amongst their peer group. Maybe they could comment on their decision to take up a more unusual instrument in addition to the piano and the guitar. For example, if they had decided to branch out and learn to play the ukulele or piccolo. This would be even more impressive if they had taken it upon themselves to find out more about their unusual instrument – maybe using YouTube or a podcast to learn more about it and to teach themselves to play it with confidence.

I've learnt to unicycle! I saw a clown at the circus last year and it looked like a lot of fun. I asked for a unicycle for Christmas and although it was really difficult at first, I carried on trying and now I can go ride it without wobbling for quite far distances.

This is a great answer as initially it is clear that the impetus for learning to ride a unicycle has come entirely from the child rather than an interest that has been imposed on them or cultivated by the parents. Having admired the skills of a circus performer they wanted to have a go themselves. At this point the support of the parents becomes clear as they listen to their child and respond to their wishes. What is even better in this response is the fact that when the child received the gift at Christmas, they found it very difficult at first to master the technique. However – crucially - they did not give up. They say that they 'carried on trying' – they did not give up at the first sign of failure. By continuing to put the effort in to learning how to keep their balance and to coordinate their limbs, ultimately, they mastered the skill. The reward was the fact that they can now 'ride it without wobbling'.

This student has faced disappointment in their early attempts to master the skill of riding the unicycle. What is impressive is their perseverance, the fact that they continued in their quest to become better. This is a quality much to be admired and would make a good impression on the interviewer. In addition to their determination and the fact that they carried on practicing, there is the reward which comes from the fact that they manage to eventually, after much hard work and effort, learn to ride a unicycle confidently 'for quite far distances' – a feat not many could say they can do!

An excellent answer.

I would say my thought processes are unique. I'm not afraid to explore different areas and some subjects spark off an interest which I like to follow up. I think to be honest; every person is unique in their own way – we might appear to be a mass of people, but everyone is different and special for who they are.

This is a very considered response. The child initially concentrates on what aspect of themselves they consider to be completely their own, apart from other people. They land on the concept of their own thought processes, talking about how they think in a different way to everyone else and that they enjoy following these thoughts up. This comment indicates that they are not limited by the path shown to them but that they are willing to explore further. They mention that some subjects 'spark off an interest'. This suggests that they may have come across a topic in the classroom which they then put time at home into learning more about it. What is commendable about this response is that the child continues with a more perceptive remark. The realisation that everyone has their own personal thoughts, ending with the fact that we are all 'different and special' for who we are. This understanding of the self and ability to take a view of other people in this manner is very mature, indicating a child who is reflective and contemplative.

When asking the candidates what they feel is unique about themselves, the interviewer is hoping to learn something more individual about them, something which will make them memorable and make them stand out from the many candidates being interviewed for a place at the school. A student who is able to think about their own attributes, achievements and personality in relation to other children and excited to identify something special about themselves will come across as happy in their own skin. Ideally, they will convey an idea about their own skills and attributes as well as an underlying indication of their attitude to learning. Are they keen to learn about something new? Have they taken the steps to do so?

There are many ways in which the child may approach this question. They may reveal more personal information, such as the fact that they have battled a serious illness in the past or that they have been involved in a police chase. Others may interpret the question in a more literal manner, talking about a birthmark or referring to a quirk in their eating habits as something which makes them different to their peers. When preparing for this question, the key thing is for the child to imagine the conversation from the interviewer's perspective. What impression do they want to leave with the interviewer? Do they want to give a jokey answer? Are they willing to be open and to share something more personal about themselves? Once the child has considered the impact they want to leave, this will inform the way they approach this question and will help them to formulate their response.

What personal achievements are you most proud of?

This is an open question with a wide range of answers available. The candidate could relate to specific achievements at school, whether academic, sporting, creative etc. The best answers will respond to the adjective 'personal' – what do they feel most satisfied with. It could be something simple such as learning to conquer a fear of the dark. In this case, the child would have been brave to admit to such an anxiety, but they are also able to discuss what strategies they put into place to conquer their worries and possibly able to explain how this achievement has affected their life positively. They may instead choose to focus on an academic milestone such as when they mastered the recitation of a poem in front of the class or learning how to complete long multiplication sums.

A poor answer.

I felt really proud when I learnt to jump into the deep end of the swimming pool. I was always afraid of hitting the bottom and sometimes I would get teased about it, especially at swimming pool parties. Now I just jump in with the others and it's fine.

Learning to dive into water is an impressive skill. In this instance, however, the child is concentrating on jumping into the water. This indicates a fear of the water, especially deep water. Their ability to swim is left unknown unless the interviewer decides to ask some follow up questions. The difficulty with this answer is the child's use of the word 'learnt'. They present the idea of jumping into deep water as a skill. Instead, what they have done is not master a new skill but screw up the courage to follow an activity their friends have successfully demonstrated to them. The student refers to their friends teasing them, which begs the question, what was their response? Were they confident enough in themselves to stand up to the ones making comments? Did they shrug the words off or were they deeply affected by the teasing?

The biggest issue here is the emphasis. The child is not highlighting the fact that they have conquered a fear of deep water. They are suggesting that they have acquired a new skill which is difficult to achieve – that of jumping into the water. The reality is that they have grown in confidence and have followed the example of their friends. Once they had taken the first jump, all others would have followed easily. This could have been a good answer if the student had changed the focus a little onto their pride at conquering their fears rather than presenting it as a big physical achievement.

<u>A good answer.</u>

I wrote a poem during Writing Club at my school and it was published in an anthology – we bought copies for all my family and friends. I feel very proud to be a published author.

In this answer the child reveals that they attend an extra-curricular club at which they have worked on producing their own creative work. The fact that they have applied themselves sufficiently to produce a poem is great. However, the child is not to know that the anthology they have been published in is not necessarily a mark of ability. Many companies now run competitions which school children are encouraged to enter, and huge numbers of their poems or stories are included in anthologies. The school generally is offered one to have in their school library and the company makes their money by the well-intended family of the pupils purchasing the anthology. As you can imagine, this can be a lucrative business and a more unscrupulous company will accept any work submitted.

In order to make sure your child's work is appreciated, it would be useful to take a copy of their poem to the interview or to take the anthology itself. The interviewer would then be able to view the work themselves and to appreciate the effort and spirit displayed. The child also has the opportunity at this point to discuss the content of the poem, suggesting what inspired them or talking about the techniques they chose to include and what effect they intended them to have on the reader. This could be a very good answer if the child is able to show their work and to talk about it, otherwise the interviewer is left to decide for themselves how much prestige they would attach to a child's work being published in an anthology which may not come from a very reputable source.

<u>An excellent answer.</u>

Last month I achieved grade 7 flute. I feel very proud because I only took it up as an instrument three years ago and it was my choice. I already played the piano and violin and I wanted to add the flute because I love the sound I can create. It feels like my own achievement which I feel very proud of.

This student displays an element of individuality which an interviewer would appreciate. It is clear that they must be musically gifted, with that ability being nurtured by the parents who have created the first opportunity by engaging a piano and violin tutor. What is interesting is that the pupil has developed their interest off their own initiative, asking to add a third instrument and choosing it themselves. They are able to articulate their reasoning and to explain what appealed to them about learning the flute in particular. It is great to see that the student's parents have fostered this request and enabled the process by supporting their choices, thus revealing a strong family dynamic which would work well for the school. This type of family is likely to be very supportive of the school environment and to encourage their child to take advantage of all the opportunities which may be offered.

The fact that the child has also managed to reach grade 7 standard within three years suggests a high level of musical ability together with the fact that the child must have worked hard and applied themselves to regular practice sessions in order to reach such a peak. This suggests that the pupil is not one to take hold of an idea for simply a few weeks or months, get lazy or indifferent to the instrument and refuse to practice. This child is excited enough to apply themselves for three years, in addition to the work they have been doing to improve their piano and violin playing skills as well. This aspect of their personality is very appealing and would come across very positively.

A student may choose anything to mention in relation to this question. It may not be related to school at all – they may be proud of when they rescued their sibling from a pond they had fallen into or feel proud of the time they helped their parent put up a trampoline. Their choice of answer will reveal a lot about themselves, showing what they consider to be something worthy of being proud of. This is a chance for the candidate to discuss what they feel has been an achievement, possibly as an individual or maybe as part of a team effort. They could reference the fact that they are part of the successful school team taking part in a cross-country competition which they came second for across their county. Maybe they are proud of a mural which has been painted on the walls of a local subway which they have contributed to. This would show an element of community spirit and would show that the child is keen to be part of projects that do not necessarily revolve around their own individual input.

An interviewer will be excited to hear the child's response in terms of their own interpretation of the word 'proud'. What might they feel truly proud of and would like to share with someone else? What makes them feel good about themselves and pleased to discuss with another person? This is their chance to give an insight into their own personality, revealing their own sense of worth and value, indicating what they feel is considered an achievement worthy of praise from another.

If you could meet anyone in the world, dead or alive, who would you most like to meet and why?

This question demands some consideration from the candidate. There are so many responses to choose from, it is definitely good to have the opportunity to consider this question at leisure, giving the answers that spring to mind some real thought. This is another question which reveals something about the child, indicating their hopes for the future, suggesting which attributes they admire, who they might like to emulate. After the initial decision is made, the student should then take some time to think about what it is about that person that they admire. Is it something they have achieved? Did they overcome some kind of adversity? Is it an aspect of their personality they are drawn to? The pupil needs to be able to identify the quality of their role model that attracts them and be able to articulate confidently to the interviewer their reasoning. One way to make this process easier is to ask the child to think about what they might hope to learn from this person. This is an easier question to answer as it is more targeted and may lead to a lengthier discussion about the person in question and why they hold them in such high esteem.

The worst answer would be if the child couldn't think of anyone they wanted to meet, or simply named someone with no real reason to suggest why they wanted to. The key to answering this question successfully is explaining the reasoning behind the decision – what is it the child hopes to gain from meeting this person? Why do they admire them? What skill or personality trait do they hope to emulate themselves?

A poor answer.

I think I'd like to meet Charli D'Amelio although she lives over in America. She's a really big star on TikTok – she has over 151 million followers and she's rich now. If we met up, I'd do a dance routine with her and she'd probably record it to put on her feed which would make me famous!

This child has chosen a celebrity mainly because they are famous. The influencer Charlie D'Amelio became popular when she put her dance videos on TikTok, and she branched out to launch perfumes and clothing items as well as taking part in commercials. She can certainly be admired for her business sense and the way she has built her career, but this child seems to be admiring her simply for her fame and the fact that she is so popular over social media combined with the fact that she is wealthy. The student is clearly hoping that they might also become famous by association if they are featured on the influencer's channel, and possibly aspire to be a social media star themselves. It is much more difficult today to become successful for posting videos on YouTube or TikTok because there are so many people doing the same thing. Obviously, there are specific dangers in young children doing so (which is why there are age restrictions on access to such sites), but many parents do not recognise the problems in allowing their children to watch these short clips. It is not the videos themselves that cause problems but the perception of the children that it is easy to become rich and famous by posting their lives online. It is a shame to have a role model who is leading a life they are unlikely to be able to emulate.

A good answer.

I think King Charles is someone I would like to meet. He's the king of our country and would be able to talk about all the places he's travelled to and people he's met. I would like to know how he feels about having so many people being interested in how he lives and being in the paper all the time.

Initially, this answer may seem similar to the previous one. The difference is in the detail of their answers. The first child seems to admire Charli for her fame and money whereas the second does not mention the wealth and fame of King Charles but focuses on the man himself. This child shows an understanding in leadership – referencing the fact that Charles in the recognised king of our country regardless of whether they support the monarchy or not – he still is held up as a leader and well-known figure who is recognised around the world. However, in addition to understanding that King Charles is a prominent member of our society, the student also mentions the interest people have in the lives of the royal family. As the head of that family, obviously the scrutiny of Charles is at its most harsh.

The child is obviously aware of the dominance of the royal family in the news and the fact that they comment on being interested in how the members cope with the pressure of media scrutiny at all times reveals a mature understanding on the part of the child in empathising with the demands placed upon those people. They are also interested in what they could find out about King Charles in terms of the people he has met himself and what he might have learnt from them – being a king, the suggestion is that he must have met a plethora of very different individuals the world over and have some insights worth sharing.

<u>An excellent answer.</u>

I've watched quite a few programmes with Professor Mary Beard, and I'd find her really interesting to meet. I'd ask her about her studies and find out what she's focussing on right now.

This student has chosen a well-known figure from the academic world, one who is respected and upheld as a great scholar. Mary Beard is not looked up to for her personal attractiveness or her way of life but for her knowledge and understanding. As such, to choose such a person as someone to meet suggests the student is thinking of what they could learn from her as a gifted intellectual. Rather than focusing on the popular media stars of the pop world or an influencer who relies on their looks or crazy antics to get views and therefore raise money, this child wants to meet a professor who they are enthusiastic about learning from. This indicates a depth of character as well as a possible interest in the professor's field of study as well. If pressed, they may well reveal that they have been inspired to conduct their own further research into the specialist subject discussed on the tv programme or podcast.

The choice of person the child would like to meet reflects on their own interests and aspirations. If they choose from among those whose fame is likely to be fleeting, this could indicate a child who has rather surface interests themselves. A decision to ask for a meeting with a well-respected person held in a higher esteem would reflect better on them. Having said that, it could be that they can explain why exactly they are attracted to that particular person and wish to ask to meet them. For example, I once asked this question of a student who replied that they would like to meet Katie Price. I was rather surprised, bearing in mind that this celebrity is commonly featured in the media due to her cosmetic enhancements and public behaviour. However, on delving a bit deeper, the child explained that they admired how she had come from a relatively poor background and admired the way she made money by manipulating the media and giving them the pictures and stories they wanted. It wasn't that she admired Katie Price the person as such, more that she respected the way she seemed to have a clear business plan and followed it through, while being clear that she had no desire to follow in her footsteps. It was one of the more unique choices I heard of and her ability to explain her choice worked well.

Afterword

This collection of interview questions is by no means complete. There are often questions relating to current affairs, which are designed to establish how much knowledge and interest the child has in events outside of their own personal bubble of experience. They may ask for views on particular issues such as the move to going paperless in schools or how much value they feel educational trips add to the student experience. However, the interview process is not based on a child's ability to comment on outside events or their part in the world around them. The main purpose is to establish what kind of a personality they have, whether they are enthusiastic and confident and what they may bring to the school themselves as well as what they may take away. Each school wants to ensure they have the best cohort attending each academic year and they want to offer their expertise and opportunities to the students who they believe will benefit the most from what they are given

In addition to focusing on the child's answers, it would be a good idea to also pay attention to their physical demeanour. They should be aware of how they present themselves to the interviewer in terms of appearance and body language – remember it has been established that many people make up their minds about another person within seconds of meeting them. If the child presents with a smart appearance, a straight posture and confident stance they will make the best possible first impression which they can them build on over the course of the interview.

I wish you all the best as you support your child on their educational journey. Remember that the experience should be a positive and encouraging one for them, it is an opportunity to present their best qualities and to convey a sense of their unique qualities within the interview process.

Printed in Great Britain
by Amazon

56545125R00026